Keys to
KINGDOM
RESOURCES

SHAWN BOLZ

Eight Keys to Kingdom Resources in Heaven's Economy
Copyright © 2015 by Shawn Bolz
All rights reserved.

Unless otherwise marked, all Scripture quotations taken from the New American Standard Bible, Copyright © 1960, 1962, 1963, 1968, 1971, 1972, 1973, 1975, 1977, 1995 by The Lockman Foundation. Used by permission. (www.Lockman.org)

Scripture quotations from THE MESSAGE. Copyright © by Eugene H. Peterson 1993, 1994, 1995, 1996, 2000, 2001, 2002. Used by permission of Tyndale House Publishers, Inc.

Scriptures taken from the Holy Bible, New International Version®, NIV®. Copyright © 1973, 1978, 1984, 2011 by Biblica, Inc.™ Used by permission of Zondervan. All rights reserved worldwide.

www.zondervan.com The "NIV" and "New International Version" are trademarks registered in the United States Patent and Trademark Office by Biblica, Inc.™
Scripture quotations taken from the Amplified® Bible, Copyright © 2015 by The Lockman Foundation Used by permission." (www.Lockman.org)

Editing: Sally Hanan of Inksnatcher
Cover Design: Yvonne Parks
Interior Design: Renee Evans of Renee Evans Design

First Edition, 2015 ISBN: 978-1-942306-25-2
Printed in the United States of America.
Publisher: ICreate Productions, 225 South Chevy Chase Drive, Glendale, CA 91205, www. bolzministries.com

OTHER BOOKS BY SHAWN BOLZ
The Throne Room Company
Keys to Heaven's Economy
The Nonreligious Guide to Dating and Being Single
Translating God

# KEYS

TO KINGDOM RESOURCES

The thief comes only in order to steal and kill and destroy. I came that they may have and enjoy life, and have it in abundance (to the full, till it overflows).

JOHN 10:10

I have heard it said (and have said myself) that Heaven has an economy. A better statement is that Heaven is full of the best economic principles in existence. God is all about economics and resources; He created everything, and He planned for it to work best within His wisdom and governing principles. Many believers separate God from economics, business, governing, resources, etc. because we don't view these things as being particularly spiritual. Christianity has long put out a message that the common things of life are not spiritual, when they are actually the proving ground for the Heaven we all ascribe to. The beautiful thing about God is, He loves His goodness and wisdom to be seen in the most common places.

I love how the Bible is full of examples of how we thrive as we get to know God and His heart, not just emotionally or spiritually, but in our natural lives as well. We also read how to practice the principles that build this lifestyle. Consider Adam and Eve, who were given dominion over all the earth. They named animals and began a stewardship process that was cut short. Their jobs were not employees to a CEO of Heaven, but of ruler-ship with God to govern and manage the resources of creation. This kind of lordship feels natural to humanity—we are the only species that builds past our instincts and natural desires. We build civilization with vision that comes from God.

The whole world, and even creation, is waiting to see what Heaven's architecture looks like in society. What does this transforming wisdom feel like when it's rooted in a business, a stock market, a creative project, or even a city planning meeting? God wants us to thrive in the midst of Heaven's wisdom and Heaven's economy, but there are keys to staying in this blessed life. To thrive is not just about us continually living a blessed lifestyle; we are here to demonstrate what our relationship to God and His Kingdom looks like in all aspects of life and society. As Christians we are wired to the feeling of satisfaction and fulfillment that comes from both enjoying and using our prosperity to impact and help this world connect to the love of God.

Christianity is spreading. When it spreads in sudden bursts of salvations, we call this revival. What if a billion people were to get saved in one generation? It could be the most profound thing that ever happened in history, but in order for it to happen, there has to be an abundance of resources and provision stewarded by Kingdom-minded people.

CREATING RESOURCE AND WEALTH
God wants you to steward great resources more than you want to.

It is He Who gives you power to get wealth, that He may establish His covenant which He swore to your fathers, as it is this day.

DEUTERONOMY 8:18

God gave the Jewish people the amazing ability to steward

wealth and finance so that people know He is with them. This didn't end in some story in the Old Testament; there is still a redemptive thread woven through the Jewish community 'til this day. Guess how many of the top bankers in the world are Jewish? Out of the top 400 positions, at least 200 are of Jewish descent! A *60 Minutes* study reports that up to 60 percent of the decision makers in the film and TV industry as being Jewish. There is still a redemptive blessing and purpose on the Jewish community around the world.

How does this relate to you? God's blessing of the Jewish people throughout history is a picture of God's desire to entrust His people with resources and wealth for the purpose of building something on the earth. This is something He is investing in humanity. When Jesus went to the cross, the Father prepared an inheritance of people for Him—an inheritance that is going to take a large gathering and maturation of resources. Therefore, you and I are going to have to become a people of great resources.

Have you heard the prophecies of the great coming harvest? It will take billions of dollars to reach a billion people. This isn't just a bare bones revival; this is a transformational work. People are going to look like the bride of Christ.

His bride has prepared herself. She has been permitted to dress in fine (radiant) linen, dazzling and white—for the fine linen is (signifies, represents) the righteousness (the upright, just, and godly living, deeds, and conduct, and right standing with God) of the saints (God's holy people).

REVELATION 19:7-8

His bride will know who she is and she will know how to partner with Jesus (the white linens represent her maturity). This means we are going to have salvation, education, and transformation in the Kingdom.

Think how much the education system costs, just in each

of the American states. According to the 2013 NASBO state expenditure report, 25 percent of most taxes collected go to the K12 school system (in most states). If God is literally bringing a kingdom to the earth, don't you think He will provide the resources so we can grow and be educated in it? He is going to invest His resources into this just like any good king, dictator, or president would.

In other words, there is a provisional plan from Heaven for each area of growth promised. If it's supposed to be developed here, God has already provided the resources to develop it and the people to govern its development. We have conceded this leadership to others for too long, but it's time for us to influence these roles, or even to occupy them.

THE JOHN 10:10 PROMISE OF ABUNDANT LIFE

Jesus's promise that we would walk in abundant life (see John 10:10) includes emotional, spiritual, and economic prosperity. In the thousands of successful people I have interacted with, there have been eight keys that seem both scripturally important and vulnerably present in those who seem to walk in a John 10:10 paradigm. These keys are practiced, it seems, not only out of character and conviction, but as a way to express love and relate to God.

Much of our Christian devotion and experience of prayer is wrapped around the idea of giving God a portion of time each day, which is valuable, but God's not an apportioned God. We are really tied to His heart through the ongoing behavior and choices we make, and these help us to connect deeply and stay present in His heart.

Consider Proverbs—a book of wisdom that helps you thrive in your relationship with God, yourself, your spouse, your family, and the world around you. It teaches that devotion to God cannot be lived through prayer time alone. Wisdom has to be a lifestyle, one that puts the world's wisdom to shame—not because the world isn't wise, but because God has a glorious, higher, deeper, and beautiful plan that only Christians can discern consistently. Wise Christians can be deliberate about bringing Heaven's plans to the earth.

EIGHT KEYS TO HEAVEN'S ECONOMY

I've put together a list of eight keys to guide you into the ongoing development of this deeper connectivity to God's plans and how to relate to Kingdom resources with a Kingdom perspective.

KEY  1

GIVING AND GENEROSITY

We make a living by what we get, but we make a life by what we give.

WINSTON CHURCHILL

Generosity is the backbone of Christianity. For God so loved the world that He gave His most precious possession: His Son. He modeled that to have true happiness and connect deeply with Him, we must be willing to practice giving as a way of life, not just to give some things when we feel like it.

Jack Welch, one of the most famous business personalities in history, was asked recently how he knew when someone was ready to be promoted to senior leadership or management. He responded, "I look desperately for the generosity gene. A characteristic of people who love to see others promoted, love to see others grow, love to see others' ideas come out and don't ever steal them. You will do so much more for the people who care about your career and have your interests at heart."

Think about those to whom others want to entrust themselves to and follow. Christians should be at the top of your list, mainly because they should understand generosity to be a central tenet of our faith's lifestyle; it keeps us present and connected to Jesus. So many well-known business and church leaders I know have shared that generosity plays a pivotal role in their lives. Generosity not only keeps you grounded in your love for others, it helps rebalance your personal values.

Jesus talked about laying down our lives, about being extravagant servants. The Bible is full of promises for those who live a generous life. One of my favorite chapters is Isaiah 58, which lists twenty-six blessings you will have if you live a generous life toward the poor. This seems to be one of the easiest keys to see, but one of the hardest to keep doing; however, it has direct fruit every time.

Then shall your light rise in darkness, and your obscurity and gloom become like the noonday. And the Lord shall guide you continually and satisfy you in drought and in dry places and make strong your bones. And you shall be like a watered garden and like a spring of water whose waters fail not.

ISAIAH 58:10-11

Giving keeps our hearts present in what we are giving to. Consider your own personal health journey: If you were paying for one of the nicest gyms in your area, your heart would stick with your health journey even if you weren't able to go for a month. Why? Because you'd be paying a price to be in shape. That investment, that tying of your resources to healthy living, would incentivize you to make different dietary choices. With every temptation, you would be challenged with the possible violation of your monetary investment and eating unhealthy food would be hard. Without the investment, the incentive to actually work out or eat right wouldn't carry as much weight.

PRESENT WITH GOODNESS THROUGH GIVING

We live a generous life because it makes us present with the issues we give to, but also it makes us present with the reality of goodness and godliness. I know a Christian billionaire who has done so much good that presidents and leaders of countries call him before they make major decisions. He told me that the key to his popularity wasn't that he was a billionaire; it was that he had generously given of his time and wisdom to help solve problems that certain nations' governments couldn't fix or create a plan for. As a result, they now look to him for advice. Generosity opened the door to national influence.

HOLD THE KEY

Here are some ways to hold onto the key of generosity:

1. Consistently give gifts that benefit the neighborhood, people, and land you live in.

2. Have a giving plan for all your loved ones' major holidays and birthdays, so that through your consistency and generosity you are staying present in their lives.

3. Be connected to key people in your industry and city. Honor their most precious projects with financial donations. Even a little giving can help people see that you honor them and are on their teams.

4. Tithing helps us to live in the value system of the Kingdom—we take a portion of what is ours and give it, outside of our control, to God. There are so many reasons to tithe, and most people who don't like to (because of frustration with theology) find excuses to give less rather than more. It's not like paying taxes, because you have no idea if they are being used properly or with corruption. Tithing has a direct tie to God despite who we tithe to, and it will always yield a result in our lives (and hopefully in a major way to the organization or community we are tithing to).

5. Give to issues of extreme poverty or injustice. This always keeps the key in your hand because it causes you to balance everything you are doing against a greater reality. Issues can ground you, whereas when you only focus on yourself, your efforts, or even your business, you can forget the central purpose of your prosperity.

KEY

FINANCE, RESOURCES, AND TIME

Money is only a tool. It will take you wherever you wish, but it will not replace you as the driver.

AYN RAND

Finances and resources are such a huge key to Heaven's economy. When you have finances and resources, your purpose on this earth can be accelerated. Some people get frustrated with this, and there is a whole generation trying to figure out how to obtain or accumulate resources without seeing a great release. God is the God of resources, and He wants to help us out of survival mode and into accumulation mode.

Money is a terrible master but an excellent servant.

P.T. BARNUM

Before I define this key, I want to acknowledge the two types of people who read this. One will feel empowered, while one will find it hits a sensitive spot. I believe the sensitivity to this is because so many people in the middle class and below have a hard time accumulating money, and as a result have a financial wound combined with misunderstanding and even judgment in their hearts when finances are talked about in Christian circles. Some people have identified with poverty for so long they have accepted it as their personal truth. You never want people who have a financial wound or poverty mentality to be the ones who dictate how to live a healthy financial life. Success breeds success but lack often breeds people of poverty.

I encourage people to go through basic financial management classes, or at minimum take a program into your home like Financial Peace University. Or get some counseling or prayer to come into an accumulation and successful mindset. Both are great starting points for people who have hit a wall.

You must gain control over your money or the lack of it will forever control you.

DAVE RAMSEY

DOLLARS AND CENTS

A key to Heaven's economy is to have resources and money. The world is looking for the people who hold these keys to answer big questions and help with huge problems. Finances are an accelerant to solving problems. As a matter of fact, this is the primary way that the Western world solves its problems: by throwing money or resources at them. We know that most problems are a lack of relationship, so what happens when we use relationship + resources to solve the problem? We get a solution grounded in permanence.

Two of our dear friends are a couple named Eric and Jodi Hannah, a director and producer. They have used their movie-making gift to create a film and then show it through their humanitarian cause, Lift Up America, which has a goal of touching underprivileged kids and creating inside of them the ability to influence through compassion. How successful have they been at using their resources and gifts to touch kids? According to their reporting:

"Through our partners, a total of $94,297,700 of college scholarships, hearing aids, and protein was given away, plus additional millions of dollars more in Gifts in Kind including eyeglasses, food items other than protein, T-shirts, DVDs, batteries, stadium seats, refreshments, and dental supplies".

I have watched the Hannahs through the years, and they seem so rare to the humanitarian world that everyone is trying to figure out how they did it. The truth is, the love for the kids in their hearts motivated them; they sought out great wisdom; they had the resources of their skills; and they had their spiritual connection with God. All of these created a historic charity cause that is one of the most influential of its day.

God says He loves the whole world, and the world is asking for that love to be proven. Finances and resources help us to father the world back into God's heart.

RESOURCE CREATES RESOURCE

It takes money to make money.

ANONYMOUS

Resources create resource and finances create finance. It sounds so simple, but one of the ways we hold this key is to create resources and finances in our lifetime and try to multiply them.

Many Christians only make enough to last their lifetime, so they aren't thinking of risking, investing, multiplying, and leaving a real inheritance. Some of this comes from bad theology—every Christian generation thinks it's the last, so we don't live for our children's children. It is time to live as though we will be here forever but hope that Jesus will return tomorrow. This will create an incentive, both ways, to be faithful with the resources God has given us for this world and for Jesus.

It's not how much money you make but how much money you keep, how hard it works for you, and how many generations you keep it for.

ROBERT KIYOSAKI

The world around us is waiting for people who have the resources and connections to finance growth. Producing the resources that solve society's problems, or using your finances to build futures for cities, is how we will disciple the nations.

I asked a friend of mine, a city mayor, what he needed from the Christian community? He said: "We are grateful for community service, but we spend a lot of money and time on event planning. We really need people who can create community, who can be a resource rather than a requester of it. We need people who the city can look up to in business, education, and media—people who share their lives, resources, and time to make this city great. If we had that, we would be the greatest city on the earth."

A CULTURE OF FATHERING AND MOTHERING THE WORLD AROUND US

I live in Los Angeles, and it's the city that everyone comes to to take from. Everyone wants something from my city. If you are an entertainer, you want to become famous; if you are a student, you want the best school; if you are a business person, you want your piece of the pie. This gets multiplied by Christians more than helped by them. We also have an entitlement attitude when coming into many things. Even the American dream can be built on entitlement: the idea that if we work hard enough we deserve a great life. We are not supposed to be only looking out for ourselves though, to take. We're also to love our neighbor as ourselves, to give. This is the difference between being in a family as a son versus as a father.

I remember going to the mayor of Hollywood's commencement speech, and during it he signed a piece of paper saying, "I may be a mayor of this great city of Hollywood only once in my lifetime, but I am signing an adoption paper with this city, and I will be a father here as long as I live. I will love it like it's my own." This had a profound impact on my heart, because if you adopt your city, your industry, and your people group as if they are yours, then you will love them as you love yourself. You will make huge sacrifices and want to use your resources to build their greatness.

The world is looking for fathers and mothers, not just believers. The world around us is waiting for us to mentor them by example, not just doctrine. We need to model giving and generosity by giving to our families, and in doing so we become inspirational fathers and mothers to the world around us.

TIME

Even before you have wealth or great natural resources (like properties or equipment the world needs), you have time. It is, in all essence, the most important commodity. You can value the poorest and the richest in society with time if they want your time.

God shows one of His highest values toward us with time. He is omnipresent and eternal but chooses to manifest Himself in the midst of our timeline to honor us with His love. He is present with us so we can be present with the world around us. Time is one of our greatest commodities. The more successful you get, the more precious your time becomes.

Time is so precious that the more successful a person is, the easier it is to feel valued by his time because you know his time is precious, unlike that of people who aren't in a position of authority or (assumed) value. In other words, if the pope works at a soup kitchen one night, the kitchen staff will use that as a sign of their value and tell everyone around, for the rest of that soup kitchen's existence, that the pope felt they were worthy enough to serve there one night. We need to value others with our time.

KNOW YOUR OWN VALUE

If you don't value your time, neither will others. Stop giving away your time and talents. Value what you know and start charging for it.

KIM GARST

When you know how to value yourself and your time, people feel greatly blessed to be prized with it. I remember two fine artists in our church who painted pictures during worship. One was a hobbyist trying to turn into a professional, while the other teaches art classes and has an amazing reputation as an artist. One Sunday each one sold a painting. I went to the two houses that held those paintings that week. The first one I went to was the new home of the hobbyist painter's picture. The artwork was sitting in the kitchen leaning against the counter (close to the trash). I asked them if it was the hobbyist's picture, and the new owner of the painting confirmed it was. She was a woman who had never bought a painting before, so she hadn't known how to value it. When she went to the artist and asked how much it would cost to buy, the artist was afraid of her own value of her art, her time, and her money that went into the painting, so she said, "Whatever you feel comfortable paying." This woman gave her $25 and walked away with the painting excited, but when she got it home, she didn't really see anywhere to hang it. I saw lots of empty walls that it would look good on, but it had turned into a novelty item to her and she wasn't even sure she wanted to keep it. I knew that the supplies the painter had used cost close to $75 because it was a mixed-media piece.

The second house I went to held the painting of the successful painter, which was already the main feature in their dining room. I asked about it and the purchaser said, "I have never bought a painting before, but I was in love with this one! I asked the painter, Janet, how much it was and she said $2,000! I was shocked because I didn't know how much art normally costs. I wanted it still, and I told her I couldn't afford that much.

She prayed about it and offered it to me for $750. Can you believe it? I have a $2,000 art piece sitting on my wall. Isn't it beautiful?"

I knew what I was seeing in the two houses was the difference of a mindset. Janet knew her college, her experience, her training, her thousands of painted pictures meant she could value her artwork at a certain price, and she had even gotten appraisals of her work to prove it. The other artist had a masters in fine arts, hundreds of paintings, and had even done gallery shows, but she was afraid of her own ability and was too insecure to have it appraised.

If we don't value ourselves, then the people around us will not know how to value us either (unless they are experts). Be your own expert and help the world relate to you so that when you have time to give or consult, it will be highly valued. I know one counselor who charges $400 an hour, but when he takes on the occasional client at a $200 discount, he values him ten times as much because he knows the counselor normally costs $400. Creating incentive by knowing what you are worth helps the world around you respect and value your time.

KEY

FAVOR, RELATIONSHIP, AND INFLUENCE

Divine favor causes you to rise to the top in your sphere of influence, and the reality is that favor can be recognized more easily if you start at the bottom.

BILL JOHNSON, FACE TO FACE WITH GOD

Favor is one of my favorite keys to Heaven's economy because it is when God sets us apart that people notice us or connect to us, even though we might not be the best or most qualified. I have seen people with favor win the interview over everyone who was more qualified. I have seen others with favor get the film contract, even though there was another company that had already proven itself more.

Favor is the one key we need to recognize and ask God for. Favor in its essence is not just charm or popularity; it is birthed out of wisdom, like the wisdom Solomon asked for to discern God's heart. When he had it, favor followed. That is what we need: this discernment of God's heart that brings about a connection to others, one that wouldn't have come if we hadn't had our relationship with God.

The Old Testament and New Testament are filled with stories of the people of God making connections with others through their relationship with God. It was only because of it that they had their breakthrough. As Christians, we are not looking to build self-serving relationships, but we know the more we connect to others the more purpose there is in the connections. The purpose of relationship is twofold for a Christian: The first reason is to expand our community and love well the people God loved first. Being present in that is huge and should never violate the second reason: to help each other go further in God. Even when people aren't believers, the people you work with will revert to your value system as you serve them if you are constantly promoting relationship.

Influence comes from our abilities, favor, education, knowledge, and wisdom, but it can also be a spiritual addition to our natural qualities. In other words, when we are developing a life in God, we have the opportunity to not just be limited to our own relational sphere of authority, but to have God's sphere of authority as well.

Joseph had so much favor from God on his life that wherever he went, he was always put in leadership positions, even in prison. Influence and favor help us lead and connect in a greater way. The Jewish people all throughout history have prayed the prayer:

The Lord bless you and keep you; the Lord make His face to shine upon you and be gracious to you; the Lord lift up His countenance upon you and give you peace.

THE PRIESTLY BLESSING, NUMBERS 6:23-27

They are praying that God gives you abundance, blessing, and favor with others, and makes you the one everyone wants to do business with or follow.

I had one friend who was a struggling actor whose agent let him go. He was desperate and felt like only God could help him. He had no more connections but knew he wasn't done with his career in the entertainment industry. In between looking for work as a free agent, he would often reach out to homeless people on skid row and give them food, not because he was part of a program, but because he loves well. The last man he spent time with one particular day was a real character. He asked if he could eat with him and as they shared a meal (a homeless man and an actor), the man said to him, "What do you need in life? You helped me; I want to help you."

My friend said, "You don't have to give me anything."

"I know I don't, but I want to. What do you need?"

"I need an agent really bad," he said, not expecting anything, just voicing frustration.

"Oh! You are a great actor! I have something for you," and the homeless man searched through his wallet and handed my friend a dirty bent card. "Call this number and talk to Dave and he will help you. Tell him I sent you."

My friend had no faith in the card but was sincerely amused, and he thanked God for the encouragement. God spoke to his heart and said, "Aren't you going to call the number?" To which my friend said, "No, it was sweet, but this can't be real." He couldn't get the question out of his head though. He had to call.

A man answered and he asked if it was Dave. It turned out to be someone in one of the top agencies in town—one he had tried to get into several times. He told Dave how he came to get the card. Dave immediately wanted to meet with him. He told my friend, "The man you met was one of the most talented agents in history, but he lost his family to a car accident, left everything, and became an addict. We all love him, but even more, we trust his opinion every time. You, my friend, are our newest client." And he hired him on the spot.

I love favor! Through it, Abraham got Sarah; Joshua got a promised land; Joseph saved his family; and Esther saved the Jews. Favor is a mystery and only comes by relationship with God, but it's a must!

KEY

HARD WORK

It takes as much energy to wish as it does to plan.

ELEANOR ROOSEVELT

Key number 4 is one that only half of the Christians I know understand. Hard work isn't supposed to be seasonal but a way of life, and we learn to rest in between. We get to work hard because we get to produce both natural results and spiritual fruit, which should drive us on all the more.

Unfortunately, many Christians are looked at as lazy, always trying to find a shortcut, and entitled. These three things should never be in anyone's vocabulary about us. We have the opportunity to see some of the greatest transformation on the earth today. We aren't just working to accumulate or to build our own lives, which is already still amazing and worthwhile; we are working for the glorious achievement of seeing Jesus get His full reward.

This key to Heaven's economy is such a strong one. People who are rich, famous, and leaders in their industry or political leaders all work hard. They do not want to relate to someone who is halfhearted or lazy. They want to see those who produce great results from hard work, and they give instant respect to someone who has a life culture of hard work.

I'm a great believer in luck, and I find the harder I work, the more I have of it.

THOMAS JEFFERSON

WORK ETHIC

I feel like believers often times live in dog years. We accomplish seven years worth of life in one human year. When we become Christians, we are constantly growing. Our activities get richer and richer as we pursue our faith in God. In the same way that someone with a doctorate would probably never go back and work for a fast-food restaurant, a mature Christian can no longer be satisfied to just use work as a means of provision. Work takes on a profound purpose to him because it's part of how he gets to connect to his destiny in Jesus. I love that Paul said (in Galatians 4:19): I work with all this energy that Christ be formed in you.

A new survey from AtTask conducted by Harris Poll found that US employees at large-sized companies (1000 employees or more) only spend 45 percent of their time on primary job duties. This is the way of the world; there is no determination to accomplish fullness. We have a "just enough" attitude, which means we do just enough to get the bare minimum done. I think this is why Daniel and Joseph were so easy to promote: They saw the big picture for the kingdoms they served and worked to see God's dream and heart manifest towards those people groups. They didn't rest in a partial day; they were blessed and favored because they lived every day to its full capacity.

Slack habits and sloppy work are as bad as vandalism.

PROVERBS 18:9 MSG

In our society we have a gap between workaholics and those who just put 45 percent of effort into their jobs. There is a way to put 100 percent of effort into doing a good job through hard work and still have great boundaries for family, rest, and hobbies. Christians get to model this because we are some of the only people who can keep these boundaries intact, thanks to our friendship with the Holy Spirit, our wisdom of reading the Bible (which helps us to thrive), and our spiritual betterment journey.

All hard work brings profit, but mere talk leads only to poverty.

PROVERBS 14:23 NIV

Whether it's a stay-at-home mother who never rests, or a business owner who works tirelessly at his passion, you can tell the difference between hard workers and slackers immediately. Successful people will never stay connected to those who won't work hard.

It is time for us to stand and cheer for the doer, the achiever, the one who recognizes the challenge and does something about it.

VINCE LOMBARDI

One of the greatest parables in the Bible is the parable of the ten talents. It is a completely spiritual parallel between our work effort and our connection to our King. Do we love what He loves? If so, we will work hard at multiplying what He gives us. If we are not afraid of disappointing Him, then we will bury our lives in lesser efforts.

Twenty years from now you will be more disappointed by the things that you didn't do than by the ones you did do.

MARK TWAIN

KEY

CREATIVITY

Creativity is one of the greatest keys because it reveals the nature of God. Whether it's the creativity to build what is in God's heart, or a creative project, or just ingenuity in an industry, creativity simplifies and connects God to humanity and makes him known in the clearest way.

ELEANOR ROOSEVELT

Then Moses said to the Israelites, "See, the Lord has chosen Bezalel son of Uri, the son of Hur, of the tribe of Judah, and he has filled him with the Spirit of God, with wisdom, with understanding, with knowledge and with all kinds of skills—to make artistic designs for work in gold, silver and bronze, to cut and set stones, to work in wood and to engage in all kinds of artistic crafts. And he has given both him and Oholiab son of Ahisamak, of the tribe of Dan, the ability to teach others. He has filled them with skill to do all kinds of work as engravers, designers, embroiderers in blue, purple and scarlet yarn and fine linen, and weavers—all of them skilled workers and designers."

EXODUS 35:30

Bazelel and his creative contemporaries had the ability to create anything that was needed for Israel to worship God and connect His heart on earth. This is such a beautiful picture of God gifting people with creative abilities so He could be known and seen. This isn't just for fine artists and poets. Creativity is how God first revealed His nature. Genesis 1:1 says, "In the beginning He created." As we begin to identify with God personally, we will start to find that the Creator not only lives in us; He created us to be powerful in our own creativity.

The world needs ingenuity and creativity. So much gets recycled in music, advertising, business models, educational systems, etc. when people don't engage creativity. Creativity can change every aspect of society and relationships faster than even policy and education can. One creative picture can instill hope, like the famous picture of soldiers holding up the flag during a tumultuous time in American history.

Creativity is just connecting things. When you ask creative people how they did something, they feel a little guilty because they didn't really do it; they just saw something.

It seemed obvious to them after a while.

STEVE JOBS, CO-FOUNDER OF APPLE

Creativity is just the process of connecting things already inside us through our Creator in a way that makes us the most present with creativity. This key to Heaven's economy has a biblical pattern and God Himself is a representative of what it looks like. He created the whole world full of resources that would last until His Son's coming, resources that would not only last but that could be cultivated into mini pictures of what eternity is like. Whether it's our relationship to animals, resources, government, or the environment, creativity brings about the personality of God's original design and helps us to become a fuller world.

Oftentimes in our Western or even Greek-minded thinking, we separate noncreative and creative people so we are not responsible if we don't think deeply about source, inspiration, and creative process. Some of the greatest minds in history were not artistic, but they were all creative.

Creativity and innovation are about finding unexpected solutions to obvious problems, or finding obvious solutions to unexpected problems. We should use our creativity to provide better businesses and solutions rather than constantly trying to disrupt what people are doing.

REI INAMOTO, CHIEF CREATIVE OFFICER AT AKQA

Creativity marks all of the changes and transitions in the world. When the writer of Ecclesiastes wrote that there was nothing new under the sun, he was referring to what humanity can bring to the world. Humanity has a lack of extreme creativity without God. Add Him and it's like a nuclear reactor of creative thought and a quantum computer of ideas.

KEY

EDUCATION

You are always a student, never a master. You have to keep moving forward.

CONRAD HALL

One of the main reasons why education is so important is because God wants to move us forward toward His goals for humanity. The whole world can feel there is more and wants to get there, but it gets stuck in its current state. Education helps us to see past our present point and pulls us into God's original plan for us, which can accelerate us toward our future.

People who aren't growing, and don't meet the world's standards of understanding and knowledge, are often looked down upon as not only unintelligent, but disconnected. I remember being about to speak to a roomful of PhD theology students, and the professor was worried that I wouldn't be intellectually stimulating enough because I don't have a PhD. After I spoke the class debated some topics with me, and we talked about theology around the world. When we were done the professor said to me, "You are a highly educated person. In my book you are on par with a PhD educated person." It was the nicest thing a highly educated person has ever said to me, although it's not entirely true. I was glad he and the students felt fed by me, but I realized how much more I need to grow, not only to be relatable to the world, but to help those around me also grow.

I also spent time addressing a college class, here in the US, during which we were talking about the growth and sustainability of African nations. I had a great perspective, but it was not married to the bigger picture and the research knowledge that it takes to stand in great authority on the issues. As a matter of fact, I sounded more like a mom-and-pop shop do-gooder then someone with authority to actually address the issues. It was sad because I had a lot to bring to the table, but my own lack of priorities was holding me back from being completely relevant.

We are responsible to become knowledgeable, and some-times experts, on different subjects, because we can connect knowledge to the solution faster than those who don't have the Spirit of God living in them. We owe the world a debt of love, and part of love's expression is a knowledgeable picture of how things should work.

We are comfortable believing in the spiritual without a goal of it changing the status quo in the natural. An example: A pastor friend of mine was praying for his city to be cancer free through the healing power of God. Because he had heard one of the fathers of the faith praying that in Redding, California, he wanted to pray it for his city. I told him I was praying for a cure for cancer too, and even praying that the main cancer research institutes would have breakthroughs in our generation that would obliterate cancer. He replied that he would only pray for the healing anointing for his church because he didn't know anything about what God wanted to do in cancer research, but he sure knew He wanted to heal cancer there. It sounded righteous to him, but it sounds uneducated to the greater Christian world, and even beyond.

His prayer was noble, but he couldn't even relate to the fact that in our Christian theology—which he agrees with—God hates disease. God doesn't just want to bring healing; He wants to give the power to create health and destroy disease. Many Christians are so focused on spirituality outside of this present world that they are of no effect in our current condition. God so loved the world, not just His heavenly realm. He was very practical in giving Adam and Eve roles. I think most Christians wouldn't even go to the problem of collecting species of animals if they were to build an ark like Noah today. They would be more concerned with the mission than the world.

EDUCATED PEOPLE ARE MORE LIKELY TO CHANGE AND TRANSFORM THE WORLD

The only person who is educated is the one who has learned how to learn and change.

CARL ROGERS

People who are educated most likely know how to grow and change. They can't stay satisfied in one-dimensional lives; they are always transforming.

We need to be the change agents of the world. We need to help the world come into God's design or plan, but to do that we have to be educated, relatable, and knowledgeable. I love that Paul was so educated in Roman religion that he was able to address them about their created idol to the unknown god. The biblical figures we aspire to be like may have sometimes started out uneducated, but they became masters of history, theology, politics, etc. so they could help steward the world around them. As we go on the journey of education, we have to literally not just try to master a subject, but stay open to being a student—a child—the rest of our lives.

The thing about God is that there is always a deeper place to know Him in, an advancement in our faith, a new glory to build on past glories. The world is moving forward at a huge and fast pace, and those who understand it become kings. I love that the

Hebrew culture values learning and knowledge, and that people express it through deep spiritual life wisdom.

It is amazing to me when some people start coasting off past advancements or achievements. If you want to have a key to Heaven's economy that will take you all the way to eternity in a thriving life, you need to keep changing and growing.

Education is the most powerful weapon which you can use to change the world.

NELSON MANDELA

KEY 7

RISK AND FAITH

I am not sure who coined it, but I love the old saying: Faith is spelled R-I-S-K. It's the Father's good pleasure to give us the Kingdom, but it's impossible to keep it coming without the faith that pleases Him. A lot of people have a hard time living a lifestyle of risk because of their fear of the occasional failure. In her book *Daring Greatly*, Dr. Brene Brown talks about how shame destroys our vulnerability. She defines vulnerability as uncertainty, risk, and emotional exposure. She also defines vulnerability as the leading trait that brings connectivity to the world around us.

To be vulnerable is counterintuitive to much of the current culture around us because of the amount of shame woven into our society. Read anything by Dr. Brown and you will grow in your understanding of what I am talking about, but know that if you do not have vulnerability, you will not take great risks. Where there is not great risk there is limited reward.

We like to be right, we like to win, we like to gain and not lose, but the reality is, everything that we do that matters will be risky. We might fail in a temporary situation, but that failure doesn't define a believer; it actually gets used in our lives as a rung in our ladder to climb toward the greatness that Jesus paid for. To be people who are okay with our failures and believe that they are not our end but just part of the process is amazing. To believe that God works them for our good is supreme. Risk is one of the keys to Heaven's economy because there is never a flow of resources and finances that doesn't have some measure of risk to it. We will at times make mistakes, while at other times other mistakes will cause us pain. Our job isn't just to power through but to be real with its effects on us, to let God heal us, and then let Him set up His divine scenario of working our lives back into the full destiny He's measured for us.

Fortune sides with him who dares.

VIRGIL

I love that the average millionaire in America goes bankrupt on average 3.5 times, according to Stanley and Danko in *The Millionaire Next Door: The Surprising Secrets of America's Wealthy.* That is crazy! That means there is no great reward without great risk!

As long as you're going to be thinking anyway, think big.

DONALD TRUMP

Faith allows us to enter into a mindset described in Ephesians 3:20: We start to look beyond what we can hope for or imagine and believe that God has something no human life can bring on its own. We are called to a divine purpose in this world, and that means in our practical life as well.

You know your mind is renewed when the impossible looks logical.

BILL JOHNSON, FACE TO FACE WITH GOD

So many people in the world are crippled by fear. It causes such an opposite reaction to how we are supposed to live. There is no way to enter into the greater purpose God is calling you to when you are driven by fear.

When you accept that you may fail, you can accomplish anything. Fear can be so debilitating. Every day I'm faced with difficult decisions, but losing the fear helps me make the right choices.

LINDA KAPLAN THALER, CHAIR OF PUBLICIS KAPLAN THALER

KEY

INTIMACY WITH GOD

I did not add this key just out of duty. It is truly the greatest key. The closer you get to God, the more you will know His mind and heart. This even translates to having direct knowledge of stock markets, policy, education, commerce, film, television, family, etc.

The worst thing we can do in life is to have a relationship with God that brings nothing to this world. That would be a very shallow relationship indeed.

A.W. TOZER

Your life in God translates to impact on the people around you. We are called to shine from the very highest hill God can light us up on (see Matthew 5), but if we don't have Him as the oil in our lamp, we won't burn for very long.

Relationship gives us the desire to build. When a young man gets married, he is thinking about how he can work to support a growing family. It is no longer just his own life but the life of many that he is providing for. Relationship with God is the same—when you enter into intimacy with God, you start to see the big picture of how to build that relationship, which gives you staying power through the ups and downs of life. When you have intimacy with God, you can hear His heart and get reset internally every time you deviate from what you are hearing. Relationship is a beautiful thing because a man will do anything to protect and build for the one he loves.

If you make history with God, He'll make history with you.

BILL JOHNSON

Interpretation: If you develop a history with and become intimate with God, just like King David did, God will make history with you. God will co-labor with you in making history. I love this quote by Bill Johnson, because God is calling for friends who really know how to stay connected to Him in everything they do. This connection is a lifeline of divine ideas, power, inspiration, problem solving, and reward. I think the reason why some people compromise their walk with God is because they haven't developed an intimacy worth protecting.

THE JOY SET BEFORE YOU

Part of developing this intimacy will cause you to fall in love with those God is in love with, and that will cause you to have a different result in your stewarding of God's economy.

I have a friend who is one of the most prophesied over individuals I have ever known. He is constantly prophesied over about the music industry, which he is in. He has been told by major leaders in the body of Christ that he will be a famous musician, fill stadiums, have songs on the radio on top charts, write with the greatest, and you know what? He can see it in his heart and spirit. One day he came to me as a friend and said, "Shawn, I have all these words; I know what my destiny is but I feel disconnected and blocked from it. There is a huge gap between what I am doing now and what I am believing for."

I could see the answer in front of me. I told him, "You think your destiny is to be on the radio, filling stadiums, and writing love songs. These are wonderful things you get to do, but it's because you are going to reach all those people who come to the stadiums, listen to the radio, and fall in love to those songs. Fall in love with the people who are your destiny instead of the calling, which is to do stuff to get to the people. You thought that your destiny was to work, but your destiny is to love."

He loved the answer and went away to pray. For months he pictured the people that he gets to love through music and fell in love with them, and after having so many years of disconnect, within only a few short months he had full connection and everything amped up and multiplied.

The writer of Hebrews said (in Hebrews 12:2) that for the joy set before Him, Jesus endured the cross, meaning He was willing to pay any price for those He got to love, and He paid it. We need to see our destiny as the people we get to love, and to connect our hearts in intimacy both to God and to those we love so that we will pay any price. This causes our calling to accelerate, because once you put love in the equation, everything will happen. Another way to put it is in the Scripture:

But seek (aim at and strive after) first of all His kingdom and His righteousness (His way of doing and being right) and then all these things taken together will be given to you besides.

MATTHEW 6:33 AMP

Steep your life in God-reality, God-initiative, God-provisions. Don't worry about missing out. You'll find all your everyday human concerns will be met.

MATTHEW 6:33 MSG

ABOUT THE AUTHOR

Shawn Bolz is the author of *The Throne Room Company*, *Keys to Heaven's Economy: An Angelic Visitation from the Minister of Finance*, and *The Nonreligious Guide to Dating and Being Single*, and he is also an international speaker, pastor, and prophet.

Shawn has been a minister since 1993, and these days he is well-known for his strong prophetic gift and fresh biblical perspective. Shawn taught, ministered, mentored, and prophesied at Metro Christian Fellowship with Mike Bickle in the '90s, and in the early 2000s he joined the International House of Prayer in Kansas City. After leaving Kansas City in 2005, he founded and still pastors Expression58 in Los Angeles—a mission base and church focused on training and equipping Christians, encouraging the creative arts, and loving people in the entertainment industry and the poor.

Shawn is a board member and representative of The Justice Group based in Los Angeles, California, with whom he has worked on social justice issues and missions operations around the world. He and his wife are also the founders of Bolz Ministries—created to inspire and empower God's love around the world—and iCreate Productions—formed to produce exceptional media that motivates and transforms culture.

Shawn currently lives in Los Angeles, California, with his wife Cherie and their two beautiful daughters.

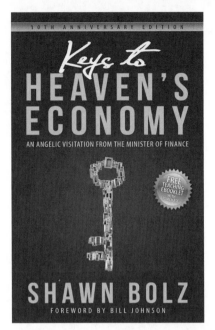

KEYS TO HEAVEN'S ECONOMY

So begins the unfolding of Shawn Bolz's
visitations from God's heavenly
messenger, His minister of Finance.

Heavenly Resources have only one
purpose–that Jesus Christ would receive
his full reward and inheritance in our
age. Just as God held nothing back
from Solomon, who longed to build a
tabernacle for God on earth, God will hold
nothing back from a generation of people
who long to bring Jesus everything
that belongs to Him!

God is about to release finances
and resources to reshape the Body of Christ
on the earth. God is looking for those who
desire an open-door experience with
the One who is the Master of all keys, Jesus.

Keys to HEAVEN'S ECONOMY
E-COURSE

DISCOVER THE KEYS TO UNLOCKING YOUR DESTINY

WWW.BOI7MINISTRIES.COM

EXPLORING THE
PROPHETIC

BE CURIOUS WITH SHAWN BOLZ

WILL FORD
APOSTLE GUILLERMO
JAMES KRAMER
MICHAEL MCINTYRE
BILL JOHNSON
KAREN GIBSON
ANTONY ARIS-OSULA
DOYIN LAYADE
PHIL SMITH
BRIAN HEAD WELCH
TOMMY GREEN
EDWINA FINDLEY
SARA BOWLING
SEAN FEUCHT
AMY WARD
MATT TOMMEY
BOB HASSON
CINDY MCGIL

BO
LZ
PODCAST

PROPHETIC ECOURSE 101

WITH SHAWN BOLZ

AN IN-DEPTH
STUDY OF THE
PROPHETIC